Special-o-saur Dinosaurs

MY ROARING
SNEAK-A-PEEK BOOK

STEP BACK IN TIME

Millions of years ago, long before the first humans, we roamed the planet. We were a special type of reptile - very special indeed!

We lived during the **MESOZOIC ERA**. This era is split into three 'periods': the Triassic, Jurassic and Cretaceous periods

But where are we now? Gone. Extinct!
Our time ended when a giant meteorite smashed into Earth
66 million years ago, killing most of the life on the planet!

DINO PIONEERS

I’m **EORAPTOR**.

I’m **PISANOSAURUS**.

When? In the Triassic

I'm **HERRERASAURUS.**

We are some of the first dinosaurs to roam Planet Earth. We early dinosaurs aren't giants like some of our later cousins.

ANCIENT LANDS

Our world looks quite different from yours. At first, all the land is clumped together into one big continent called **PANGAEA**.

But slowly Pangaea is torn apart, with each piece of land taking its own set of animals with it.

We bask in warm weather, even at the poles! We walk between the ferns, cycads and conifers and see Earth's first flowers bloom.

SAFETY IN NUMBERS

Most of us live in **HERDS**, big or small. We make sure to leave footprints in the mud so that, in years to come, you can count how many of us there are. You're welcome!

SIMPLE BEGINNINGS

No matter how big we end up,
we dinosaurs are all born from an **EGG**.
Some eggs are as small as a chicken's egg,
while others are as big as a football.

SUPERMUM

I’m **MAIASAURA**
and I’m a great mum!
My nest contains up to 40 big eggs
and I care for every single one.
I look after my little ones
long after they’ve hatched.

When?
In the late
Cretaceous

SMALL AND AGILE

I'm **COMPSOGNATHUS**.
Don't be fooled by my size.
I may be no bigger than a turkey,
but I'm a fast and agile hunter.
So watch out!

When?
In the late Jurassic

I'm **EPIDEXIPTERYX**.
Watch your step!
I'm as small as a pigeon, but
I have much prettier feathers!

When?
In the late Jurassic

GIANT AMONG GIANTS

I'm **PATAGOTITAN**, the biggest land animal E-V-E-R!

(Or at least that's what they say...)

When?
In the late Cretaceous

And how did I get this big, you might wonder?
By eating my veggies... all day long. Yum!

SPEEDY SPRINTER

I’m **GALLIMIMUS**, the rapid racer!
Like a giant ostrich, I run on my two hind legs.
I could compete with a galloping racehorse,
if any lived at the same time as me.

When? In the late Cretaceous

NO-RUSH-DINO

I'm **ARGENTINOSAURUS**.
I don't run. I'm much too big for that.
And everyone is sure to get out of the way
when they hear my giant footsteps, so
there's no need for me to hurry, anyway.

When? In the early Cretaceous

KNIGHTS IN DINO-ARMOUR

I'm **SAUROPELTA**!
Think twice before you
pick a fight with me.

I'm **ANKYLOSAURUS**,
but you can call me the king of clubs!
My tail has a bony club to smash with,
my head and cheeks are all spiky and
I'm covered with an armoured
back plate.

When?
In the late Cretaceous

My armour is nice and strong,
and watch out for my long shoulder spines.

When? In the early Cretaceous

SHARP HEADED

I'm **TRICERATOPS.**
I can hold my own in a fight thanks to my fancy neck frill and three horns. Attack me if you dare!

When? In the Cretaceous

I'm **STYRACOSAURUS**.
I have a super-long nose horn.
And check out the horns on
my tall neck frill. How about that!

When? In the late Cretaceous

PRICKLY PAIR

I'm **KENTROSAURUS**.
The row of double plates starting at my neck become impressive spikes the further back they go. And don't forget my long tail and shoulder spikes!

When?
In the late Jurassic

small, but not
ook at my plates - all
pout my spiked tail?

SUPER SAIL-ORS

I'm **OURANOSAURUS**.
Sure, Spinosaurus is tall, but I was r
a sail long before he was even born.
And I only eat plants!

Ahoy there! I'm **SPINOSAURUS**. Thanks to the two-metre-high sail on my back, I'm the tallest of all meat-eating dinosaurs!

When?
In the late Cretaceous

BIG-HEADED DINOS

TOOT! I'm **PARASAUROLOPHUS**, a duck-billed dinosaur.
My head crest steals the show.
People think I use this long tube as a trumpet...
but I like to keep them guessing!

When?
In the late Cretaceous

SMASH! I'm **PACHYCEPHALOSAURUS.** I'm a peaceful plant-eater, but if someone wants to butt heads, I'm ready! Check out my thick, dome-shaped helmet covered in fancy knobs and spikes.

When? In the late Cretaceous

BITING BEAKS

I'm **BARYONYX** and I love fish – chomping them between my teeth, that is! My long snout is perfect for fishing.

And with my nostrils set high, near my eyes, I can keep breathing while I fish.

When?
In the early
Cretaceous

When?
In the Cretaceous

I'm **PSITTACOSAURUS** and I love salad. Some say I have a tortoise-like head with a parrot-like beak. I also have small horns on both my cheeks!

TOP TAILS

I'm **DIPLODOCUS**, the friendly giant.

I'm **CAUDIPTERYX**, your little feathered friend! Like a peacock, I have a fan of feathers at the tip of my tail.

But I'm only friendly if you are - if not,
I can snap my extra-long tail like a whip.

When?
In the late Jurassic

When?
In the early
Cretaceous

CLAWSOME

I'm **THERIZINOSAURUS**.
Don't be scared - I don't eat animals, just plants. I'm very tall, with a long neck, a small head, feathers...

When? In the late Cretaceous

and super-long claws. In fact, they are all anyone seems to notice! Sure, they might be the longest claws ever, but I won't use them to hurt you.

PLANT-LOVERS

Most dinosaurs only want plants on their plate.

I'm **BRACHIOSAURUS** and, like most giant dinosaurs, I'm vegan.

When? In the late Jurassic

I'm **PROTOCERATOPS**. I use my horny beak to nibble at plants.

When? In the late Cretaceous

I'm **IGUANODON**.
My large thumb spikes help me fight off meat-eating predators - but as for me, I love my greens!

When? In the late Jurassic and early Cretaceous

MEAT-EATERS

Some dinosaurs prefer a bonier dinner.

I'm **TYRANNOSAURUS REX**, the king of the dinosaurs. I can gobble up a smaller dinosaur in a single bite!

When? In the late Cretaceous

I’m **OVIRAPTOR**.
I may not have teeth, but watch out
– I use my powerful beak to bite!
I’ll eat almost anything, from meat
and eggs to bugs and plants.

When? In the late Cretaceous

FLYING PTEROSAURS

I'm **QUETZALCOATLUS.** As the largest flying animal of all time, I cast quite a shadow. Just imagine a giraffe with wings!

When? In the late Cretaceous

I'm **DIMORPHODON**.
I have a short body,
but my head is long,
bulky... and full of teeth.

When? In the early Jurassic

SWIMMING PLESIOSAURS

I'm **ELASMOSAURUS**.
My neck is loooong - in fact, it's longer than my body and tail combined!

When?
In the late Cretaceous

I'm **PLIOSAURUS**.
My bite is the strongest of all.
Even stronger than that of
T-Rex, who I could gobble up
in one go... if only we were
alive at the same time!

When? In the late Jurassic

DINOSAUR DESCENDENTS

Who can call the dinosaurs their
great-great-great-great-great-grandparents?
Yes, you guessed it: me!
And I'm just a run-of-the-mill chicken.
In fact, all modern **BIRDS** descend
from the dinosaurs.

GONE BUT NOT FORGOTTEN

We might all be gone now, but our **FOSSILS** are still hiding in the earth and rock beneath your feet.

When these are found, dinosaur experts called palaeontologists put them on display in a **MUSEUM**. So come by and say hi!